W9-AOX-772

First Ladies

Lady Bird
Johnson

Joanne Mattern

ABDO
Publishing Company

visit us at
www.abdopublishing.com

Cover Photo: Courtesy Lyndon Baines Johnson Library and Museum
Interior Photos: Corbis pp. 19, 20, 21, 23, 25; Getty Images p. 5; Courtesy Lady Bird Johnson
    Wildflower Center p. 31; Courtesy Lyndon Baines Johnson Library and Museum pp. 6, 7, 8, 9,
    11, 13, 15, 16, 17, 18, 22, 27

Series Coordinator: BreAnn Rumsch
Editors: Megan M. Gunderson, BreAnn Rumsch
Art Direction & Cover Design: Neil Klinepier

Library of Congress Cataloging-in-Publication Data

Mattern, Joanne, 1963-
  Lady Bird Johnson / Joanne Mattern.
     p. cm. -- (First ladies)
  Includes index.
  ISBN 978-1-59928-795-9
  1. Johnson, Lady Bird, 1912---Juvenile literature. 2. Presidents' spouses--United States--
Biography--Juvenile literature 3. Johnson, Lyndon B. (Lyndon Baines), 1908-1973--Juvenile
literature. I. Title.

  E848.J64M38 2008
  973.923092--dc22
  [B]

                                                                            2007009731

Contents

Lady Bird Johnson 4

Pretty as a Lady Bird 6

Missing Mama 8

College Days 10

A Sudden Marriage 12

Off to Washington 14

Working Wife 16

New Roles 18

An Unexpected Turn 20

Beautiful America 22

Home to Texas 24

A Hopeful Future 26

Timeline 28

Did You Know? 29

Glossary 30

Web Sites 31

Index 32

Lady Bird Johnson

A First Lady can have a lot of influence in the United States. Some First Ladies use their position to better the country. They take an idea they believe in and make it a reality. Lady Bird Johnson was one of these First Ladies.

Mrs. Johnson was married to Lyndon Baines Johnson. He served as the thirty-sixth president of the United States from 1963 to 1969. During those years, America faced numerous difficulties. Many people lived in poverty or were victims of **racism**. America was also fighting in the **Vietnam War**. These issues made President Johnson's job very challenging.

Mrs. Johnson helped her husband in many ways. Together, they faced America's problems. And, they worked hard to make the United States a better place for everyone.

Lady Bird Johnson was important to her husband's success. And, her kindness and down-to-earth personality made her a popular First Lady.

Pretty as a Lady Bird

Claudia Alta Taylor was born on December 22, 1912. She grew up in an eastern Texas town called Karnack. There, Claudia spent her childhood surrounded by trees and flowers.

Claudia was the third child of Thomas and Minnie Taylor. She had two older brothers, Tommy and Tony. Thomas owned a general store, as well as a lot of land. Minnie took care of the children and their home.

The Taylor family lived in a big, beautiful house. They called it Brick House. The home was filled with books. There, Claudia loved listening to music and reading books with her mother.

The Taylors hired a nurse to help care for Claudia when she was a baby. When the woman first saw baby Claudia, she said, "Why, she's as pretty as a lady bird!" The name stuck. So for the rest of her life, Claudia would be called "Lady Bird."

Lady Bird's nurse, Alice Tittle, was responsible for her nickname. In the south, a lady bird is another name for a ladybug.

6

Thomas's business was very
successful. So, Lady Bird's
childhood home had a big yard
for her to explore and play in.

Missing Mama

When Lady Bird was five years old, her mother fell down the stairs. Unfortunately, Minnie was badly hurt in the accident and died soon after. At the time, Lady Bird's brothers were away at boarding school. So, Lady Bird was home alone with her father. She missed her mother very much.

Lady Bird and Aunt Effie depended on each other for companionship. Aunt Effie called Lady Bird "Bammy."

Thomas tried his best to care for his daughter. But it was difficult without his wife. Soon after Minnie died, Thomas sent Lady Bird to live in Alabama with her Aunt Effie. Aunt Effie was like a second mother to Lady Bird. A year later, Aunt Effie and Lady Bird came back to live at Brick House.

In Karnack, Lady Bird began school in a one-room building. There were not many other children at the school. Sometimes, Lady Bird felt lonely because she had no one to play with.

Lady Bird loved playing with animals while she was growing up.

When that happened, Lady Bird went outside. She spent hours exploring the woods, the fields, and the hills near her home. Lady Bird especially loved spending time among the Texas wildflowers. "I was a child of nature," she later said.

College Days

In 1928, Lady Bird graduated from Marshall High School in Karnack. She wanted to go to college, but she was only 15 years old! So instead, she went to a junior college called St. Mary's Episcopal School for Girls. Then in 1930, Lady Bird moved to Austin to attend the University of Texas.

College helped Lady Bird become more sure of herself. In high school, she had been quiet and shy. Now she made many new friends. She went to parties and joined clubs. Lady Bird also enjoyed attending plays during her free time.

Lady Bird was a hardworking student. She took classes for typing and teaching. In 1933, she earned a degree in history. But Lady Bird had another plan for her career. She had been working as a reporter at the *Daily Texan*, the university's newspaper. She enjoyed her job because she met many interesting people.

So, Lady Bird stayed in college for an extra year to earn a degree in **journalism**. She wanted to be a reporter and travel around the world. Lady Bird graduated from the University of Texas in 1934.

When Lady Bird began college, it cost just $25 to attend per year! And, male students outnumbered female students four to one.

A Sudden Marriage

In September 1934, Lady Bird went to visit a friend from college. While she was at her friend's office, a tall man named Lyndon Johnson came in. Lyndon asked Lady Bird if she would meet him for breakfast the next day. She agreed to the meeting.

The next day, Lady Bird arrived at Lyndon's hotel. But she was too nervous to go inside! Lyndon saw Lady Bird and ran out to meet her. They spent the day together talking about many things. Lyndon worked in Washington, D.C., and had big plans for the future. Lady Bird decided she liked this outgoing, determined young man.

Lyndon liked Lady Bird, too. He even proposed to her that same day! But, Lady Bird did not yet want to marry Lyndon. Two months later, Lyndon again asked Lady Bird if she would marry him. He told her that if she said no, he would go away forever.

Lady Bird did not want to lose the man she loved. So, she said yes. They got married the following day, November 17. At just 21 years old, Lady Bird was about to start a new life.

The couple took their honeymoon in Mexico. Then, they returned to Washington, D.C., where Lyndon went right back to work.

Off to Washington

Mr. Johnson loved politics very much. He had a job as secretary to Congressman Richard Kleberg. So, the **newlyweds** moved to Washington, D.C. Mr. Johnson met many interesting people at his job. He often brought his friends home for dinner. Therefore, Mrs. Johnson frequently found herself making dinners for unexpected guests!

In 1937, Mr. Johnson ran for Congress. Mrs. Johnson did not think she wanted to campaign with her husband. But, she found other ways to support him. Mrs. Johnson borrowed money from her family to help pay for his campaign. And, she made sure he had good meals and clean clothes when he came home between campaign stops.

Mr. Johnson won the election! Mrs. Johnson worked hard to learn about the part of Texas her husband represented. She gave tours of Washington to important visitors from Texas. And, she spoke with Texans to learn about the things they needed. Mr. Johnson discussed his plans with his wife. Then, he listened carefully to her thoughts and ideas.

Mrs. Johnson was shy and stayed in the background during her husband's campaign. But, her quiet support helped him succeed.

Working Wife

In 1941, the United States entered **World War II**. Mr. Johnson wanted to help, so he became a navy officer. He went to the South Pacific to fight in the war. Mrs. Johnson stayed in Washington, D.C., and ran her husband's office. She was busier than ever! But, she learned she could make a difference and help people in need.

Mrs. Johnson wanted to keep working after her husband returned to Washington in 1942. So in 1943, she bought KTBC, a radio station in Austin. Mrs. Johnson worked hard to make the station bigger and better. A few years later, she bought several television stations throughout Texas. Then, she launched the Texas Broadcasting Corporation.

Mr. and Mrs. Johnson enjoyed their jobs. But they also wanted to start a family. On

Mrs. Johnson learned how to take care of her family and run a business at the same time.

Mrs. Johnson was a hands-on businesswoman. She made many of the decisions that helped KTBC succeed.

March 19, 1944, Lynda Bird Johnson was born. The Johnsons had another daughter on July 2, 1947. They named her Luci Baines Johnson. Now everyone in the family had the same initials, LBJ!

Family Legacy

In 1943, KTBC in Austin, Texas, was a struggling business. But, Mrs. Johnson saw a hopeful future for the little radio station. She purchased it and spent seven months working hard to improve the station. She even mopped the floors herself! Mrs. Johnson studied how the station had been previously run and found areas to improve. Soon, the station started making money instead of losing it.

Later that year, the Johnsons added CBS, a major broadcasting company, as a news partner. This improved KTBC's popularity. By 1945, 2.5 million people were listening to music and news on KTBC! In 1973, the call letters were changed to KLBJ. KLBJ stayed in the Johnson family until 2003, when it was sold to Emmis Communications in Texas.

Very few First Ladies have had a career during their husband's presidency. But Mrs. Johnson enjoyed working. She proved that with determination, anything can be accomplished. Mrs. Johnson turned the company she purchased for less than $20,000 into a multimillion-dollar business. The company's stations remain popular throughout Texas.

New Roles

In 1948, Mr. Johnson ran for the U.S. Senate. The Johnsons traveled all over Texas. Mrs. Johnson enjoyed the campaign. She found out she liked giving speeches and meeting new people. Mr. Johnson won the election and began his 12-year career as a senator.

Mr. Johnson worked hard and became an important leader in the Senate. Sometimes he worked 14 hours a day! But in 1955, Mr. Johnson had a heart attack. He spent six weeks recovering in a hospital. Then he went home to the family's ranch near Stonewall, Texas. Mrs. Johnson cared for him until he was ready to return to work.

In 1960, John F. Kennedy was running for president. He asked Mr. Johnson to be his **running mate**. Now the Johnsons had to work harder than ever. To help the campaign, Mrs. Johnson gave

Mrs. Johnson's active role in the campaign built her husband's popularity. In 1960, he was unanimously elected as the vice-presidential candidate for his party.

speeches and hosted teas. She traveled 35,000 miles (56,000 km) in just two months! In November, Mr. and Mrs. Johnson's hard work paid off. Mr. Kennedy and Mr. Johnson won the election! Now Mr. Johnson was the vice president of the United States.

Mrs. Johnson enjoyed being the vice president's wife. She helped First Lady Jacqueline Kennedy entertain many guests at the White House. She also traveled and gave speeches. But soon, everything changed.

Mrs. Johnson helped everyone during the campaign. She hosted many events for Mrs. Kennedy, who was about to have a baby.

An Unexpected Turn

On November 22, 1963, the Kennedys and the Johnsons traveled to Dallas, Texas. As they drove through the city, someone shot President Kennedy. He died soon afterward. Later, a man named Lee Harvey Oswald was arrested for the shooting.

Now, Vice President Johnson would become president of the United States. The Johnsons and Mrs. Kennedy flew back to Washington, D.C., right away. Mrs. Johnson stood beside her husband as he took the presidential oath aboard **Air Force One**.

During her husband's campaign, Mrs. Johnson toured the southern states aboard a train she called the "Lady Bird Special."

President Johnson had many new responsibilities. And, Mrs. Johnson supported his work. The Johnsons needed to lead a country that was shocked and sad. Mrs. Johnson later wrote, "I feel like I am suddenly onstage for a part I never rehearsed."

In 1964, President Johnson ran for president. Mrs. Johnson gave many speeches in the south to help his campaign. She was very proud when her husband was elected.

Mrs. Johnson strongly supported her husband's interest in civil rights. She spoke to many people, emphasizing the benefits of racial equality.

President Johnson worked hard to help the American people. He created new laws that provided food, medical care, and money to poor families. The Johnsons also tried to help those who faced **racism**. In 1964, the president signed the **Civil Rights Act**. This law gave equal opportunities to all Americans.

A Better Life

In 1863, slavery became illegal in the United States. However, it remained difficult for African Americans to enjoy the same rights and freedoms as white Americans. Over the years, many laws have been passed to try to ensure the rights of African Americans. Yet, many white people have opposed these laws.

In the early 1900s, the Jim Crow laws made it illegal for African Americans to share buses, schools, restaurants, and even water fountains with white people. It wasn't until 1954 that the Supreme Court ruled this separation, or segregation, illegal.

The Johnsons believed segregation was wrong. So when Mr. Johnson became president, he worked hard to make sure new laws were passed. Finally on July 2, 1964, he signed the Civil Rights Act.

The Civil Rights Act worked to ensure racial equality in employment, voting, and public areas. Today, inequality continues to be a challenge in the United States. However, the Civil Rights Act made important progress toward equality for everyone.

Beautiful America

Mrs. Johnson also decided to use her position as First Lady to help Americans. So in 1964, she became active in Project Head Start. This program gave free medical care and education to children

Mrs. Johnson strongly felt that if children have a good start, they have a better chance of succeeding in life.

in need. The First Lady traveled all over America, visiting schools and day care centers. She met many children and families that had been helped by the program.

Also in 1964, Mrs. Johnson began the First Lady's Committee for a More Beautiful Capital.

She had noticed that many fields and forests were being destroyed. But now, she worked to clean up Washington, D.C.'s neighborhoods. The First Lady asked everyone to help by planting trees and flowers.

Then, Mrs. Johnson decided to spread the message across the country. As she traveled, the First Lady saw many billboards. She wanted people to see beautiful flowers instead of big, ugly signs. So in 1965, she asked Congress for help.

By October, Congress passed the Highway Beautification Act. This law limited the number of billboards that could be built. Many people called the law "Lady Bird's Bill."

The First Lady raised enough money to plant 2 million daffodils, as well as other plants and flowers, around the capital city.

Home to Texas

In 1968, America was fighting in the **Vietnam War**. The war was unpopular. Americans were divided over how the country should proceed. President Johnson wanted to end the war. However, he was near the end of his term and his health was poor. So, in March he announced that he would not run for president again. In January 1969, the Johnsons went home to LBJ Ranch in Texas.

There, the Johnsons stayed busy. They planned a presidential library. The Johnsons gathered many important papers and gifts for the project. The Lyndon Baines Johnson Library and Museum opened in May 1972. Mrs. Johnson also wrote a book called *A White House Diary*. In it, she told many stories about her life as First Lady.

The Johnsons also spent time with their family. Both of their daughters had married during the 1960s. By 1973, the former president and First Lady had seven grandchildren. They all enjoyed many happy times at the ranch.

The Johnsons outside of the newly built
Lyndon Baines Johnson Library and Museum

A Hopeful Future

Mr. Johnson continued to have trouble with his heart for many years. On January 22, 1973, he had a heart attack and died. Mrs. Johnson was very sad and lonely without her husband.

Despite her loss, it did not take long for Mrs. Johnson to get back to work. She continued to run the Texas Broadcasting Corporation. And, she was a board member for the University of Texas in Austin. She also worked for the National Park Service and the American Conservation Association. These organizations work to save America's natural beauty.

In 1982, Mrs. Johnson founded the National Wildflower Research Center. She gave a large sum of money and some of her own land to start the project. The center's goal is to save America's flowers, grasses, and trees. People come from all over the country to study the wildflowers there.

Mrs. Johnson has said the National Wildflower Research Center is her greatest accomplishment. It is a symbol of her hope to make America a better place. Lady Bird Johnson will always be remembered as a First Lady who gave of herself for the good of others.

Mrs. Johnson continues to enjoy the beauty of nature.
In 1998, the wildflower center was renamed the Lady
Bird Johnson Wildflower Center in her honor.

Timeline

1912	Claudia Alta "Lady Bird" Taylor was born on December 22.
1928	Lady Bird graduated from Marshall High School.
1930–1934	Lady Bird attended the University of Texas.
1934	Lady Bird married Lyndon Johnson on November 17.
1941–1942	Mrs. Johnson ran her husband's office while he fought in World War II.
1943	Mrs. Johnson bought the KTBC radio station in Austin, Texas.
1944	The Johnsons' daughter Lynda Bird was born on March 19.
1947	The Johnsons' daughter Luci Baines was born on July 2.
1948	Mr. Johnson was elected to the U.S. Senate.
1961–1963	Mr. Johnson served as U.S. vice president.
1963–1969	Mrs. Johnson acted as First Lady, while her husband served as president.
1964	Mrs. Johnson became involved with Project Head Start; she started the First Lady's Committee for a More Beautiful Capital.
1972	The Lyndon Baines Johnson Library and Museum opened in May.
1973	Mr. Johnson died of a heart attack on January 22.
1982	Mrs. Johnson founded the National Wildflower Research Center.

Did You Know?

Mrs. Johnson never liked her nickname, Lady Bird.

The Johnsons had a pair of beagles named Him and Her.

In 1965, Mrs. Johnson was the first First Lady to hold the Bible on which her husband placed his hand while taking the presidential oath. Every First Lady since has followed this tradition.

Mrs. Johnson's favorite flowers have always been the wildflowers native to Texas. These include bluebonnets, black-eyed Susans, daisies, and Indian blankets.

In 1972, the Johnsons gave LBJ Ranch to the United States as a national historic site.

Mrs. Johnson is one of the few living Texans with an official historical marker. It is located near the post office in her hometown of Karnack.

Coral is one of Mrs. Johnson's favorite colors. A rose of that color has been named after her. A yellow tulip was also named in her honor.

Mrs. Johnson has received protection from the Secret Service longer than anyone else in U.S. history.

Glossary

Air Force One - the aircraft that carries the president of the United States.

Civil Rights Act - an act passed in 1964 that made discrimination based on race, religion, or national origin unlawful.

journalism - the collecting and editing of news to be presented in newspapers or magazines or over television or radio.

newlywed - a person who just married.

racism - the belief that one race is better than another.

running mate - a candidate running for a lower-rank position on an election ticket, especially the candidate for vice president.

Vietnam War - from 1957 to 1975. A long, failed attempt by the United States to stop North Vietnam from taking over South Vietnam.

World War II - from 1939 to 1945, fought in Europe, Asia, and Africa. Great Britain, France, the United States, the Soviet Union, and their allies were on one side. Germany, Italy, Japan, and their allies were on the other side.

Web Sites

To learn more about Lady Bird Johnson, visit ABDO Publishing
Company on the World Wide Web at **www.abdopublishing.com**.
Web sites about Lady Bird Johnson are featured on our Book Links
page. These links are routinely monitored and updated to provide the
most current information available.

Index

A
Austin, Texas 10, 16, 26

C
campaigns 14, 18, 19, 20

D
Daily Texan 10
Dallas, Texas 20

E
education 8, 10

F
family 6, 8, 14, 17, 24

J
Johnson, Lyndon Baines 4, 12, 14, 16, 17, 18, 19, 20, 21, 24, 26

K
Karnack, Texas 6, 8, 10
Kennedy, Jacqueline 19, 20
Kennedy, John F. 18, 19, 20
Kleberg, Richard 14
KTBC 16

L
Lyndon Baines Johnson Library and Museum 24

N
National Wildflower Research Center 26

O
Oswald, Lee Harvey 20

S
social causes 21, 22, 23, 26
Stonewall, Texas 18, 24

T
Texas Broadcasting Corporation 16, 26

V
Vietnam War 4, 24

W
Washington, D.C. 12, 14, 16, 20, 22
White House Diary, A 24
World War II 16